EcoYoga

All life is yoga,

including your life.

Make it a good yoga,

through the meditations

and exercises to be

found in this book.

EcoYoga

Practice & meditations
for walking in beauty
on the Earth

Henryk Skolimowski

Gaia Books Limited

A GAIA ORIGINAL

This is a Registered Trade Mark of Gaia Books Limited

First published in the United Kingdom in 1994 by
Gaia Books Ltd, 66 Charlotte Street, London W1P 1LR

A catalogue record for this book is available
from the British Library.

Printed and bound in China by Imago

Typeset in 11pt Garamond

10 9 8 7 6 5 4 3 2

This book has been helped by many forces and many people. Among them are my students who took my EcoYoga workshops in Theologos, Greece.

In the final stages I received many helpful comments, insights and suggestions, particularly from Eric Antonov, Juanita Skolomowska and the editors of Gaia Books. To them I owe the debt of gratitude and bountiful thanks.

Henryk Skolimowski

CONTENTS

Preface   9

All Life is Yoga   18

The Yoga of Empathy   30

The Yoga of Reverence   38

Sacred Texts   48

The Yoga of Universal Karma   68

The Yoga of Silence   84

The Yoga of Listening   92
The Yoga of Empowerment   102
The Yoga of Spiritual Life   136
The Inner Springs of Life   156
Sensitivities   174
The Author   190
Other Books   191
Acknowledgements   192

To walk in beauty is not an easy task. It is like
reestablishing a perpetually collapsing bridge.
You must be forever watchful, forever aware.
The bridge of serenity does not stand firm forever.
It is like a crossing made of loose planks:
you always reassemble the planks.
It is a continually creative act. And a frustrating one,
too. You would like this bridge to be firm, but it is not.
It is a ceaselessly dynamic and
balancing activity. So enjoy the balancing act.
For there is much joy in the process of
maintaining the bridge, as there is in enjoying
its fruit: peace, serenity, radiance.

Preface

A yoga for our time must be uniquely relevant to our current situation. Traditional precepts of yoga were devised for a much simpler more bucolic world, and we now need to add other yogas to assist the health of our minds and bodies in current societies. As the world develops, we need different exercises and practices to keep centered.

In this little volume, I address myself to the inner self of the individual and offer some suggestions for relevant paths, meditations and techniques which can lead to sanity and radiance. By following these paths each of us can learn to live in dignity, with meaning and with happiness. I call these meditations and practices EcoYoga. They are steps towards Walking in Beauty.

Unlike a book of traditional Indian yogas, we are not prescribing specific postures or physical exercises, but what we offer is still yoga, a way of being at peace with yourself and the world today. The ideas and practices of EcoYoga, or the Yoga of Being, have gradually evolved out of years of reflection about the spiritual nature of the human.

Preface

There is an extremely long and valuable tradition of yoga. The great systems of yoga are a wonderful achievement of the great civilization of India. The Indian mind learned early to see the wholeness of the universe and to weave the individual into the overall harmony of the Cosmos. Many other cultures have lagged far behind.

It may be said that the Indian culture has excelled in developing the technologies of the soul while Western culture has excelled in developing the technologies for manipulation of the outside world. At their best, systems of yoga are both physical and spiritual exercises.

In the West however, yoga often seems confined to physical exercises - the body seems to be more important for Western people than their spirit. This kind of yoga alone is not enough for our times, we must recognize that personal and spiritual well-being and the well-being of the planet are interconnected.

Preface

The main focus of EcoYoga is: Grace, Health and Hope. We need to regain grace in our lives in order to make them more meaningful. We need healing on a large scale, healing of ourselves and the planet Earth. We need hope as a shining beacon to lead us forward, to guide and sustain us.

This is not a book to be read in an hour. It is a pool of tranquility to be dipped into from time to time with reverence, for spiritual nourishment, for meditation and for reflection.

> *This is a book about yoga.*
> *The main point of every yoga is not to talk*
> *about it or read about it, but to practice it.*
> *Without practice a yoga is a faint*
> *shadow of its real strength.*
> *With practice good yoga*
> *can change your life.*
>
>

How EcoYoga was Born

All life is one
great yoga.
Yoga is breathing
with the harmony
of life.

How EcoYoga was Born

How EcoYoga was Born

The German philosopher Arthur Schopenhauer (1788-1860) recognized early the substance and subtlety of the Indian tradition :

"Compared to these ancient rishis, we, philosophers in the West, are still in the kindergarten."

Perhaps Schopenhauer exaggerated a little, yet the overall conclusion cannot escape us: as its history progresses Western philosophy is becoming more and more abstract. It is not rooted in the heart and the spirit but is centered in abstract thought.

The Western ideal has become to provide a system of philosophy. It has been assumed that if this system is original and coherent, it should work by itself. It should change us by virtue of the very ideas it contains. In spite of our great philosophical sophistication, western academics and ordinary people somehow miss an important point:

Ideas expressed in a book (or just held in the abstract mind) are only a part of the story. Good ideas must become a part of our blood, so to speak, they must live in us and everything we do.

How EcoYoga was Born

This was forcefully brought home to me by a friend of mine, an actor and a director of a school for actors. After the publication of my book *Eco-Philosophy: Designing New Tactics for Living*, (1981), I had a long conversation with this man. He listened attentively as I explained the major ideas of the book, nodding his head from time to time. He really could listen well, I knew he was absorbing my ideas completely. Then he took a deep breath and asked me an unexpected question: "What kind of exercises are you going to give them?"

"What exercises?" I responded. "I am not training actors. I am a philosopher, building a new system."

He smiled gently and said pensively: "You don't understand. If you give people only ideas, they will stay in the abstract part of their coconut. These ideas will not be integrated with people's lives. You need to devise exercises which will translate ideas into living experiences, into the layers of their being so that they can live these ideas and not only think about them. Thinking about ideas is one thing. Living them - quite another."

How EcoYoga was Born

Somehow I thought his challenge impertinent. Yet deep down I felt it to be very pertinent. Indian systems of thought have historically combined reflection with yoga beautifully. But in Western philosophy there has been no such thing.

During the next few months the question would return: "What kind of exercises are you going to give them?" Finally I started devising exercises. I was already perfectly aware that thinking of the world as a huge clockwork mechanism was a big mistake of Western civilization and the source of many of our troubles. My Eco-philosophy taught me that we must look at the world quite differently, namely as a sanctuary. If the world is a sanctuary, then the most appropriate mode of our behavior in the world so conceived is reverence. Thus, we must practice reverence as a right mode of our being in the world.

Within a year the first principles (and respective practices) had articulated themselves. A year or so later, other principles fell into place. I shared these principles with others and they found these practices and exercises useful.

The Nature of EcoYoga

The EcoYoga exercises are particularly meaningful and powerful when performed in natural surroundings, preferably amidst forests and mountains, away from the tensions and noises of civilization. My favorite place is the village of Theologos, on the island of Thassos in Greece, which is for me an EcoYoga sanctuary. I hold classes there each summer.

After I developed the exercises, the need arose to publish them in a written form. At first I resisted the idea. The purpose of yoga is to practice it, not to talk about it. Yet writing is a form of sharing, and many good and valuable books on yoga have been written.

When I started writing the book, I meant it to be a simple manual explaining the various exercises. As the writing continued, the book started to change its nature. It wanted to go further and deeper. It wanted to become a guide on how to reach grace in your life, how to tune in to the great forces of the universe so that your Being shines. I have not resisted the direction the book has chosen to follow.

All Life is Yoga

Yoga is an
imitation of life.
When life performs
at its best it is most
radiant and
accomplished.

All Life is Yoga

Although yoga is chiefly associated with India, other cultures have also included many rituals and practices which connected the individual with Divinity, soma with psyche, knowledge with being.

All religions which are vibrant and alive offer a system of yoga. The rituals various religious systems offer not only bring the human close to the Divine, but also lead to the realization of the highest potential within each individual. This is also the purpose of all great yogas. If a given religion is alive, it invites you to participate, to be in touch with Divinity daily. When religion declines, its religious practices become little more than empty rituals. If a religion or a church becomes hollow, then individuals invariably seek sustenance elsewhere.

The ancient Greeks of the Golden Period cultivated their own specific yoga, although they did not refer to it as such. They conceived the body as a vessel of the inner god. Their minds were tuned to poetry and sublime discourse while they exercised their bodies, thus harmoniously combining physical and spiritual health.

All Life is Yoga

We practice yoga in order to have a healthy and harmonious body, but we also practice yoga to attain peace of mind. If your mind is not at peace following yoga practices, then your yoga is not working as it should for you.

Nowadays, in order to have peace of mind, it is vital that you establish peace with the Mother Earth. Healing the earth, so that future generations have a chance to live, is part of your peace of mind and part of the peace within your body. This is an important message of EcoYoga.

If you truly care for your peace of mind and for the harmony within your body, you cannot escape the responsibility for healing the planet. Heal the earth/heal thyself are aspects of the same process.

During the last decade a powerful new symbol has emerged. The Greek name for the goddess of the earth was Gaia. Conceived as Mother Earth alive in her total being, as the source of life, Gaia has become a new point of convergence, has emerged as a new myth of our times.

Revere the Earth

dentifying with Gaia has led to new perceptions, practices, and rituals. The overall context of these rituals is reverence bordering on worship. Thus a new religion is emerging, the religion which follows from the yoga of Reverence for Mother Earth. Its church is the entire Cosmos!

Gaia sees and

supports us all.

But she needs

our tender care,

our sense of

empathy with

her purposes.

The Journey of EcoYoga

Proposed in this book is a journey, the journey of reconnecting yourself with your inner self. You also learn to reconnect yourself with the earth, the rock, with water and with trees: these are all in you, as you have grown out of them. We practice the yoga of Empathy, or the yoga of Identification: by unifying with the elements we come closer to ourselves. This journey of empathy is also one of re-enchantment. In addition to receiving the elements and being friendly with them, we meditate on the wonders of creation. We practice the yoga of Reverence, from reverence for a single tree to reverence for all the forms around us.

As we progress we extend the reverence for the world into reverence for ourselves. You can express this reverence for yourself by recognizing that you are an exquisite piece of creation! So you learn to watch what you think, for what you think you become.

You must also be careful about what you eat, for what you eat your system becomes, and about how you spend your time. If you spend too much time on trivia, you don't have enough for important things.

The Journey of EcoYoga

We also learn to revere other human beings, particularly those around us. One way to revere others is through listening well. The art of listening is subtle and important. Listening well is a form of love.

Specific strategies of empowerment are contemplated. We find that we are made powerless in a world of highly specialized technologies, that this is a world of dis-empowerment. We are told that there is an expert for everything, and we ourselves are powerless, incompetent and unable to be our own masters. We can counter this trend and develop specific strategies of empowerment, evoking those great eras when people believed in arete (overall excellence).

Always remember, we live in the world which is a sanctuary.

We consider the meaning, beauty, and astounding powers of the Earth and its place in various yogas, especially in the yoga of Spiritual Empowerment.

The Journey of EcoYoga

We also become increasingly aware of our own relationship with the Earth, as well as our position in the entire Cosmos.

During our journey towards development we travel to the subtle realm of the yoga of Spiritual Life, questioning our relationships with the Divine, how much responsibility we bear for our own spiritual quest and how much allegiance we owe to god-within.

> *'Earth's crammed with heavens.'*
>
> ROBERT BROWNING

For the practitioner of EcoYoga, life's process is stupendous, awesome and mysterious, not piecemeal, fractured or boring. The EcoYogi's reverence for life means that every act of life matters, counts towards a greater articulation of life.

The prayer of the EcoYogi is one of attending to all our ecological and environmental realities. It is attending to the rock, earth, tree, wind and water - in order to hear God's voice calling for reverence for life, calling us to become part of this voice.

Every Act of Life Matters

The Cosmos endows us with many powers, and it is sad that we so often use them in such a meager way or with such a lack of perspective. Many of us seem to have lost the ability to recognize and rejoice in our own powers, whether they are small or great. We are all given many talents, we all have different aptitudes and abilities. We have a duty to ourselves and to the earth to recognize that every act of life matters, however small. We must acknowledge this in everything that we think and do. Our daily actions have consequences for our own future and for the futures of those who will come after us.

You can celebrate your unity with yourself and with the Cosmos. You can be in touch with the elements, and be touched by them. You can learn to be in empathy with them, by being harmoniously woven into all there is.

Life is a celebration, so learn to celebrate your healthy body and the peace of your mind. Contribute to the healing of others and the healing of Mother Earth: You can identify with the highest light and become it.

Walking in beauty does not signify
the capacity of walking on water,
but walking with your feet firmly
planted on the ground while your
eyes are fixed on the stars and
your heart compassionately
breathes with the rest of creation.
"Walking in Beauty"
is the modern equivalent for
the traditional Christian
phrase of "living in grace."

A Few Words about Meditation

Meditation of whatever form is simply a matter of mental hygiene. We are accustomed to taking care of our bodies daily: brushing our teeth, showering and washing our hair. But we are primitive about taking care of the hygiene of our minds and souls. Daily meditation, of whatever kind, is a reminder that you have a mind and soul which require attention.

In our noisy and mentally polluted world, we need to reflect on what our minds have become and how they actually function. Are you proud of your mind? Or does your mind rush frantically around, hardly ever asking why?

Take time to take care of your mind.

A Few Words about Meditation

Before you begin any exercise, sit comfortably, close your eyes, and breathe quietly for a minute or two.

Watch your breath, feel that you are getting truly relaxed.

Don't allow any tension to come into you while you are breathing, and watch your breath: in and out, in and out, deeply.

With your eyes still closed, say: "Time is my friend. I have all the time I need. Time is my friend."

Repeat this meditation before each yoga in this book.

The Yoga of Empathy

> *When you know the*
> *meaning of empathy*
> *with the elements you*
> *begin to comprehend*
> *the mysteries of life.*
>
>

The Yoga of Empathy

Let us go for a journey - if possible into a forest, or wild place. Let your mind be free. Allow time for this journey.

Try to select a landscape where there are rocks, trees, and possibly running water. If you can't go to a forest, go to a big park, or bring a piece of solid rock home. The important thing for any yoga is to be in the right frame of mind, and that you allow time. Always remember, time is your friend.

The re-enchantment of the world comes from active identification with those primordial rhythms of life whose beat you will find in yourself - if you look deep enough. Everything that is was once a rock. The earth is the same element that was once a rock but it now carries and nurtures life. There is no life without water, and trees are magnificent and powerful creations. You can allow yourself to identify with all these elements. When you understand how it feels to feel empathy with these elements you will rediscover some important elements in yourself.

Approach the rock and embrace it as tightly and meaningfully as you can. You must not feel embarrassed or shy. Your bones are made from the remnants of rocks, and everything there is was once a rock. So in embracing the rock you are embracing yourselves - in your earlier states of being. Embrace the rock as a part of yourself. You are this rock. Feel its solidity, its roughness, its texture. Feel how wonderfully enduring it is, and how it is already cracked, ready to disintegrate further to give rise to other forms of being.

Spend several minutes contemplating this rock. Look at it in a new way, as if you have never seen a rock before! See the forms of life which are already there - though hidden. Contemplate its origin, and what it wants to become. Feel yourself in this rock. A rock is a frozen spark out of which the tulips will grow. Then take a deep breath and wonder for a while longer.

Now you know the meaning of empathy with the rock.

The earth is the same element that was once a rock. You can experience the reality of the earth.

Choose a patch of ground to sit on, perhaps a bed of grass next to some soil. Submerge your fingers in the soil, and feel it. Feel it profoundly. Feel the beat of life in this earth. The entire earth is the dust of rocks transformed into life. Listen to the earth and feel its great reverberating rhythm.

Take another deep breath and wonder for a minute or two. Don't rush. Time is your friend.

Now you know the meaning of empathy with the earth. You begin to comprehend the mystery of life.

Contemplate also the simplicity and magic of water. How extraordinary it is. Think of the world without water. Can you? Now you touch the heart of mystery - the simplicity of it all, woven in one stupendous symphony.

Move to running water, ideally to a brook or a river but even a running tap will do, or a shower can be a good place. Now feel that water. Feel how fluid and wet it is. Feel how different it is from the rock, which is so unyielding, stern and majestic. Yet the water always finds its way. It goes around and about and finally dissolves the rock.

Take your time. Don't rush. Time is your friend.

Now find a tall tree. Embrace it lovingly. It is your friend. Just hug it, and breathe with it. Feel its energy. Experience the texture of its bark - how varied it is and how subtle are its colors. Smell the bark. Become one of the leaves of the tree and feel the delight of the wind caressing you. Stretch up as if you were the trunk of the tree. Feel its pulsating lovely energy.

Now you know the meaning of empathy with the tree. And you can feel what a different experience it is when you embrace a rock and embrace a tree.

Going to the Roots is your Strength

You have relived part of your natural journey. You have contemplated your beginnings through the rock and through the earth. You have experienced the simplicity and magic of water and the power of the tree.

Sit quietly, perhaps under the tree you have hugged, and reflect on the communion with the four elements. You may have strongest empathy with one or other of them, try and understand why. Can you think of reasons that you should identify strongly with certain elements and less with others?

You may be able to recognize which of the elements has contributed most to the forming of your character. Make notes about these reflections, and go over these notes in a few days. Then you can reflect on the experiences again. This is a form of your strength. Going to the roots is your strength!

Each time that you make the journey to empathize with any of the elements you will find that your empathy goes deeper and deeper until you can truly identify with each of these four elements. Take time to reach this stage, for time is always your friend.

The Yoga of Reverence

To think reverentially is first of all to
recognize human life as an intrinsic value;
is to recognize love as an essential and
indispensable force of human existence;
is to recognize creative thinking as an
inherent part of human nature;
is to recognize joy as an integral
part of our daily living;
is to recognize the brotherhood
of all beings as the basis of
our new understanding
of the Cosmos at large.

The Yoga of Reverence

If you can, you should practice the yoga of Reverence during the same session as the yoga of Empathy. After a short break, in the same natural surroundings, try to digest the experience at a deeper level. You have re-lived your oneness with the rock, and the earth, and the water, and the tree. It was a healing experience, sustaining, cleansing. You received new energies from rock, earth, water and tree. As you view the

> Reverence is a
> burning flame
> extolling all
> creation.
> ❧

world with reverence your perceptions and your mind are elevated. They are in a new space. You perceive reverentially. Your mind experiences the world reverentially. Your mind is tuned to a subtle space. That is what the yoga of Reverence is about: to behold the world reverentially, to behold yourself reverentially.

Look at the same tree again. What a wonderful chemical laboratory it is! How can a single tree do it all so effortlessly? Truly it is a miracle! Behold it as an exquisite creation and marvel at it. Take your time. Remember, time is your friend.
Then look again at yourself.

Look at yourself in a much deeper way than you have done before. What an exquisite creation you are! The tree is formidable enough. But you are a marvel of creation. And so is every human being. Let us embrace them all in a reverential hoop. This is the meaning of one human family.

Reverential Thinking

When you look at the tree reverentially and yourself reverentially you live the meaning of reverence. You need to extend this experience to the world at large. When we continually perceive and receive the world in a reverential frame of mind, we continually live in a re-enchanted world.

The state of reverence is a subtle thing, which can be difficult to attain. Therefore you have to work on it. You need to be clearly aware what it feels like to attain a reverential frame of mind. Reverence is a natural state of being which is accessible to all. There are times when we have all experienced reverence in our lives. Being in love is a state of the reverential mind par excellence. For some cultures, such as Native American Indians, reverence has always been a natural state of being - in daily reality. But although it is natural to human beings, the reverential mind only comes to most of us as the result of working on ourselves, and sculpting our minds appropriately.

It can be difficult to cultivate a reverential mind as we have long been subjected to a ruthlessly inappropriate yoga, which I call the yoga of Objectivity.

The Objective and the Reverential Mind

Thinking assumes an enormous variety of forms of which objective thinking is just one. We are not born with an objective mind. Objective thinking is not an imperative of nature, nor of God, nor of the Cosmos. It is an imperative of objective science. Objective thinking is a servant of which science is the master.

> By using our mind with reverence we re-enchant and resacralize the world.
>
> We regain our identity.
>
> We reclaim our destiny.
>
>

The objective attitude or the scientific method attempts to limit the perception of the world to what is assumed to be there, and attempts to deny what science's assumptions deny. Objectivity means clinical detachment and dispassionate forms of observation, the form of perception which atomizes phenomena that we investigate. Objectivity assumes that things exist in isolation, that every phenomenon we examine is the universe in itself, not part of a whole.

The Objective and the Reverential Mind

The yoga of Objectivity consists of a set of exercises specific to the scientific mind, exercises practiced from the time pupils go to high schools to the time they complete their university studies. It takes years of stringent training before the mind becomes detached, objective, clinical, "pure". This frame of mind is seen as indispensable for dealing with scientific facts and scientific descriptions of reality. The scientific method of describing reality has molded the mind to be its servant. The yoga of Objectivity is a gentle form of lobotomy.

Technology wants to make us into entities made of interchangeable parts, so that it can handle us smoothly and efficiently. The machine-dominated world represents the disenchanted world. Through making the mind reverential again, we re-enchant and resacralize the world. This act of re-enchantment is not a sentimental journey but a fierce act of regaining our own identity and our own destiny. The yoga of Reverence is full of blood and fire and painful re-alignments as we throw away the yoke of conditioning and regain our dignity and autonomy.

The Yoga of Reverence

Think of yourself in love; think
of the space you walked in.
It is not the space of dreams.
It is the space of reverential
reality which you create through
your reverential mind.
You need to cultivate this kind
of mind, so that more and more
moments of your life are lived
in the reverential space.

Cultivating the Yoga of Reverence

We must practice reverential perception and reverential thinking to regain and maintain a reverential mind. Reverential thinking is exactly what it states: thinking infused with reverence. Its underlying assumption is reverence for life, reverence for all living beings, for all living systems. Reverential thinking is the foundation of right ecological thinking, when the latter attempts to be truly life-enhancing.

> *'There is a*
> *spirit behind*
> *every tree.'*
> AMERICAN INDIAN SAYING

Thinking reverentially means embarking on a new set of values. Other cultures, such as North American Indians, and Buddhists, have always been able to express reverence for nature, for all living things.

Thinking reverentially must come from the heart of our being. Let us be supremely aware that to think about reverence is one thing, to think reverentially is quite another. Thinking reverentially is not just ordinary or objective thinking but the thinking that compassionately embraces the other, that tries to understand the other from within.

Cultivating the Yoga of Reverence

Reverential thinking creates a field of good energy; ultimately it is healing thinking. Reverential thinking is not a luxury, but a condition of our sanity and grace. Those who cannot think reverentially impoverish their own existence. Thinking as calculation is one thing; thinking objectively according to the requirements of science is another thing. Thinking reverentially when we behold the universe in its intimate aspects, infuse it with our love and feel unity with it, is yet another thing. And what a joy it is!

> *'There is a Buddha in every blade of grass.'*
>
> BUDDHIST SAYING
>
> ❧

Objective thinking and reverential thinking are opposites. Objective thinking recognizes no grace and values no reverence. Objective thinking creates indifferent observers, people who have little care and love for society and human beings; for care and love are excluded by objectivity. Reverential thinking, on the other hand, creates compassionate participants in the world pregnant with grace, love and mystery.

Sacred Texts

There are many ways to cultivate the yoga of Reverence. Sacred texts are important because they are reverential hymns, extolling the beauty of creation. Whether inspired by "God" or conceived by our minds in a state of ecstasy, these texts sing the power of the reverential mind which is capable of re-enchanting reality. Religion at its best is one magnificent act of enchantment of the otherwise brutal world. Great poetry is a vehicle of the reverential mind. It elevates and sends us forth, moves us up to the reverential space, and reminds us of our inner greatness.

Read some great poems and contemplate some texts which belong to sacred literature. Then you can watch the reverential mind at its high glory.

Shakespeare's 29th Sonnet

'When in disgrace with Fortune and men's eyes,
I all alone beweep my outcast state,
And trouble deaf heaven with my bootless cries,
And look upon my self and curse my fate.
Wishing me life to one more rich in hope,
Featured like him, like him with friends possesst,
Desiring this man's art, and that man's scope,
With what I most enjoy contented least,
Yet in these thoughts myself almost despising,
Hap'ly I think on thee, and then my state,
Like to the Lark at break of day arising,
From sullen earth sings hymns at Heaven's gate,
    For thy sweet love remembr'd such wealth brings,
    That then I scorn to change my state with Kings.'

from Song of Songs, The Bible

'May the wine go straight to my lover,
        flowing gently over lips and teeth.
I belong to my lover,
    and his desire is for me.
Come, my lover, let us go to the countryside,
    let us spend the night in the villages.
Let us go early to the vineyards
    to see if the vines have budded,
if their blossoms have opened,
    and if the pomegranates are in bloom -
        there I will give you my love.

The mandrakes send out their fragrance,
    and at our door is every delicacy,
both new and old,
    that I have stored up for you,
        my lover.'

From the Upanishads

'When a man knows God, he is free: His sorrows have an end, and birth and death are no more. When in inner union he is beyond the world of the body, then the third world, the world of the Spirit, is found, where the power of the All is, and man has all: for he is one with the ONE.

Know that Brahman is forever in thee, and nothing higher is there to be known. when one sees God and the world and the soul, one sees the Three: one sees Brahman...

God is found in the soul when sought with truth and self-sacrifice, as fire is found in wood, water in hidden springs, cream in milk, and oil in the oil-fruit.

There is a Spirit who is hidden in all things, as cream is hidden in milk, and who is the source of self-knowledge and self-sacrifice. This is Brahman, the Spirit Supreme.'

'Speak the truth, do not yield to anger; give if you are asked; by these three steps you will become Divine. Let a wise man blow off the impurities of his self, as a smith blows off the impurities of silver, one by one, little by little, and from time to time.

'Lead others, not by violence, but by righteousness and equity. He who possesses virtue and intelligence, who is just, speaks the truth, and does what is his own business, him the world will hold dear. As the bee collects nectar and departs without injuring the flower, or its color or scent, so let a sage dwell in the community.'

From the Shantiveda

'May all embodied creatures
Uninterruptedly hear
The sound of Dharma issuing from birds and trees,
Beams of light and even space itself.

May there abound in all directions
Gardens of wish-fulfilling trees
Filled with the sweet sound of Dharma
Proclaimed by the Buddha and Bodhisattvas.'

'The Tao flows to all places, both to the left and to the right. All creatures depend upon it for life, yet it claims no authority over creation. It does what is needed to sustain life but seeks no glory. All creatures are fed and clothed by it yet it is not their master. Small in ambition or desire, when all creatures turn to it, although not their master, yet it is truly great. Being without display, it is indeed great.'

From Mencius

'The trees on the Ox Mountain were once beautiful. However, because the mountain is on the borders of a great state, they were cut down with axes and saws, so how could they retain their beauty? Yet they continued through the cycle of life and the feeding of the rain and dew to put forth buds and new leaves. But the cattle and goats came and browsed amongst the trees and destroyed them. This is why the mountain is now bare and stripped. People look at it and think this is how it has always been. But this is not the true nature of the mountain.

And this is also the case with humanity. Surely we were not without benevolence and righteousness? The way in which a person loses their true goodness is just like the way trees are destroyed by the axe. Cut down day after day, how can the mind, anymore than the tree, retain its beauty or continue to live?'

Walking Through Nature

Walking through rugged mountains or deep embracing forests is cleansing and inspiring. What happens when we are cleansed and inspired? We become reconnected with our inner selves, we feel renewed. Forests still inspire us with awe and mystery. They are true sanctuaries. In them we can understand the idea of the world as a sanctuary in a profound way.

> '*A forest is a peculiar organism of unlimited kindness and benevolence that makes no demands for its sustenance and extends generously the products of all its life activities. It offers protection to all beings, offering shade even to the axeman who destroys it.*'
>
> BUDDHA
>
>

Small Steps to Grace

We all need spiritual nourishment. And most of us know that it cannot be received via cold rationality or scientific knowledge. Those who go through life ignoring their spirituality are deluding and impoverishing themselves. If you are stubborn and clever enough, you can deny your spiritual self forever. But why would you choose to do that? Never be less than you can actually be.

Of all the gifts of evolution, mind is the most precious. We must guard it against mental pollution. Whatever we may do to save the planet, however strictly we avoid wasting energy and ensure that we take all possible steps to recycle and conserve, these will only be half-measures as long as we allow our minds to be ruined and polluted. The fight for our future, the fight for our individual destiny is the fight for the preservation of the integrity and beauty of our minds. We are back to the yoga of Reverence.

Small Steps to Grace

The yoga of Reverence is a difficult art. But its rewards are great. Whenever you can, extend those moments of your reverential perception and thinking further and further. Walk in beauty, until finally you reach a state of living in grace. To achieve this state is to become a sublime being. You can then help others because your problems are resolved - you have reached your own core. Even if you only approach this state, it is worth all the time, exercise and discipline. Thus you should look at your acts of discipline not as an unnecessary pain but as small steps leading to grace.

Remind yourself from time to time what a mystery life is, what a wonderful piece of work you are. Look at the world you live in and have the courage to exclaim to yourself:

What an amazing world I live in!
What a fantastic spectacle to witness!
What an incredible journey!
May I be grateful to Life for its gifts.

The Beauty of Your Mind

'To see the World in

a grain of sand,

And a Heaven in

a wild flower,

Hold Infinity in the

palm of your hand,

And eternity in

an hour.'

WILLIAM BLAKE

The Beauty of Your Mind

In our present situation we are literally bombarded all the time with new information, whether we want it or not, whether it is important or trivial. Unfortunately it is often trivial. Never in the history of humanity have people been subjected to such a barrage. We take in more and more. But every human organ has a limited capacity to take and hold.

The capacity of the human brain is phenomenal, but not limitless. In theory we should be helped by the accumulation of an enormous mountain of knowledge. But in fact we easily become confused and incoherent because our minds are overloaded by trivia and turned into wastebaskets. As we let so much trivia into our minds they become cluttered and then suffocated by useless and unnecessary knowledge.

Mind is indeed the source of bondage and also the source of liberation.
To be bound to things of this world: this is bondage.
To be free from them: this is liberation.

The Beauty of Your Mind

We are the sculptors of our destiny through the way we treat our minds, through the way we allow them to thrive, or by inhibiting their flourishing. We sculpt ourselves through our own thinking. But we can also be sculpted by others - through the ways they influence and manipulate our minds.

We need to ask ourselves some important questions. Do we realize how much we are being manipulated by others, particularly the media? Most of us praise ourselves for being individualist and independent in our thought. Yet most of us are like carbon copies of the views inculcated on our minds by the mass media. This is a subject for reflection, and a deeper meditation.

The insidiousness of our present media is due to the fact that they are always working on you, never allowing you a moment's reflection. This is not true freedom. This is not true autonomy. This is not true dignity. To be fully human you must have time for reflection; you must be left in peace.

Examine the views of the people around you. See how their minds often mirror what is fed into them by TV, by newspapers, by advertising? If they are so influenced, why should you think that you are exempt from this influence? So think again, systematically, and try to put in writing the various ways you have been "persuaded," or to put it bluntly, manipulated.

Just by doing this simple exercise you are beginning to become more free. For our freedom begins when we become aware of our bondage.

What are you doing to avoid mental noise, spiritual squalor, the conditions in which your life is diminished, made gray, flat, one-dimensional? Ask this question every night for two weeks, and answer it. Put your answers down on paper.

Review your notes periodically. This is yoga. Then design strategies to combat the pernicious influences. By avoiding these negative influences you can find ways to make your mind shine with positive energy. Practice the ways which enable and encourage your mind to shine.

Universal Karma

We are responsible for what
we think and how we think.
We are responsible for the countless
forms of action we perform.
Through them we sculpt our
individual universe, through
them we are literally makers
of our destinies.

Universal *K*arma

Make Your Own Destiny

Karma is a Sanskrit term which conveys the idea that all our actions bring consequences. Bad deeds bring about bad consequences while good deeds produce good outcomes. The Christian tradition recognizes the idea: As you sow so shall you reap. This is exactly the meaning of Karma. Both in the Buddhist/Hindu, as well as in the Christian tradition, Karma has predominantly moral meaning. Morally bad deeds bring about bad consequences.

Yet the realm of Karma goes far beyond the moral universe. Everything that we do and think has some consequences on our lives and on the world around us. EcoKarma is generalized karma, born of the conviction that we are much more responsible for our lives that we usually assume. We have discussed one aspect of EcoKarma, the consequences of our thinking, of our mind's activities on our lives: As you think, so you become.

Exercising Discipline

D iscipline is part of your spiritual journey. Every spiritual exercise requires discipline. We need to build this discipline as we would build the muscles of our body. We start from easy exercises and go through training into more and more difficult ones. Patience, resilience and perseverance are vital to every person who seeks coherence in his/her life. It may be said that keeping good diet has nothing spiritual about it, but this is a very superficial way of looking at it. Keeping good diet is very much the result of subtle spiritual exercises. When you go to a food store you make conscious choices, discrimination based on a judgement because of desirable consequences in the future. This is spiritual discipline. The more often you stick to your choices and the path you have chosen, the easier it becomes to hold onto the path - whether it is by avoiding rubbish food, trivial television programs, or utterly meaningless conversations. EcoKarma or Universal Karma extends the range of our responsibilities.

As you eat so you become. We have now accept-ed this idea. We have become rather careful in what we choose to put into our mouths. We are now quite aware how the various poi-sons travel through the food chain to affect our health. Yet many additives (read: poisons) are added to our various foods. We carefully read labels and try to pick what is good. This is the right yoga of Health. The idea of health food makes perfect sense. The best of this food avoids unnecessary chemicals, is grown in season, preferably in our own region, and is grown from soil and water not saturated with pesticides. We may still not know many things about our body - for it is a miraculous organism. But what we do know obliges us to treat our bodies with respect and reverence. This of course means no junk food.

> *'Leave thy drugs in the chemist's pot If thou can't heal the patient with food.'*
>
> HIPPOCRATES
>
>

Notice what you eat and why. Reflect whether you have had any health problems in the present or in the past. Consider what part your diet might have played.

Remember: Most food contains medicinal or healing properties. It is worth finding out about the different properties of various types of foods, but if you are aware of yourself and your body you should instinctively know what foods seem to contribute to your positive health.

Reflect what foods (which you like) make you feel good. Cultivate the diet which is good for you.

Choose your Friends

Good friends are a gift to treasure, yet we need to be aware of the ways they contribute to our lives. By and large they add to our lives but not always.

You tolerate all kinds of weaknesses in your friends because they are your friends. This is how it ought to be. But it is possible that sometimes you may tolerate too much and allow friends to treat you in a way that diminishes and trivializes you... and them. Real freedom and responsibility mean that you should choose as your friends those persons who add to yourself, who stretch you and make your life more meaningful. And you should add to their lives. In helping them, in stretching them, you contribute to good Karma. It is wonderful to help others, and adds to the meaning of your life as well as adding to theirs.

> *Choose your friends with care. Good friends are more important to your life than you may think.*
> ❤

Reflect on your friendships. Which people really help you in the process of bringing more radiance into your life? Ask yourself what kind of people you should be with. And perhaps also ask yourself what kind of people you should not be with.

Make a list of all your friends' strengths and the ways in which they add to your life. Also list their weaknesses, and the ways they trivialize you. Next to these lists, write down the ways in which you add to their lives, or otherwise!

This exercise may seem very harsh, but it is very worthwhile. We must always be clear about the ways in which we are influenced, and the ways in which we influence others.

Choose your Gods

In the free world, within free market economy, you can buy almost anything that you ask for, as long as you do not request anything of real importance. You cannot buy wisdom, you cannot buy things of spiritual value.

You can ask for important things in the church, but churches today often seem to have abdicated their spiritual responsibility and have become progressively empty of spiritual content. Many people have become alienated from institutionalized religion. This is one of the reasons why Eastern gurus flourish, for they at least ask us to return to some fundamentally important questions.

In our society the important matters seem often to be economics and technology. In a sense they have become our gods. Nowadays the two modern gods of Economos and Technos have been served to the point of obsession and to the exclusion of other gods. Our liturgy has become overwhelmingly economic and technological.

Choose your Gods

The two gods of economics and technology have given us some benefits but at the price of removing us from the sources of spiritual sustenance. As with every choice we make, we have to ask ourselves which gods we can afford to worship and which gods we should avoid.

> *If your gods*
> *trivialize your*
> *existence, then you*
> *are in trouble.*
>
>

The Majesty of Life

'In splendid
majesty we just
beauty see;
With certain
vision life may
perfect be.'

BEN JONSON

The Majesty of Life

Universal Karma

Universal Karma maintains that we live in a participatory universe. But we must participate meaningfully, not trivially. We are blessed and cursed with an enormous responsibility - for everything we do and think and eat and imagine. Once we become aware of these responsibilities, we cannot ignore them. Deep down we must marvel what a beautiful thing it is that we are so responsible.

We are responsible with regard to the duties our jobs entail, as well as with regard to the laws of the country in which we reside. We are also responsible in a much deeper and more exquisite sense for all of our actions and our thoughts.

Reflection and Practice

very kind of yoga requires reflection and some practice. Ultimately, the exercises we perform are spiritual ones - their purpose is to bring us into inner balance and harmony. When we reflect on the nature of spiritual exercises in the strict sense, as performed within traditional religious orders, their purpose is similar to what we are all striving for now: avoidance of clutter and triviality. But these exercises also have a positive dimension. They help us to make sense of life, they help us to become more radiant, they help us to connect with higher purposes - through which we are elevated.

The exercises of EcoYoga are spiritual exercises for our times. We need these spiritual exercises now, as much as ever before (whether we call them yoga, meditation, ritual, therapy) for our lives tend to be swamped, torn, disconnected, and often incoherent.

Remember, time is your friend. So ask it from time to time to slow down. Then be mindful of what you think and what you eat, what gods you actually serve and why, and who you spend time with and why.

Yoga is a constant vigilance of your life - with the purpose of enriching it. You need not be shy to aspire to a higher life. This is what life calls us to do. Be the maker of your destiny! Because you are! Through everything you do.

Universal Karma

Universal Karma is mindful of
all aspects of your existence:
From food to the images of God,
from right thinking to right friends,
it is all one wheel of karma.
And you roll and roll and roll within it.

The Yoga of Silence

'Elected silence,

sing to me

And beat upon my

whorled ear,

Pipe me to pastures

still and be

The music that

I care to hear.'

GERARD MANLEY HOPKINS

The Yoga of Silence

Listening to Silence

I n the deep wells of solitude, we find inner peace, inspiration, and countless sources of creativity. All great works were conceived in silence. The silence of the desert aided Jesus in his quest of recreating human morality. The silence of the banyan tree enveloped the Buddha for days and nights as he groped toward enlightenment. Great works of art are conceived in silence before they are executed in marble, on canvas, or as lines of poetry. Great ideas are usually brooded over in solitude, sometimes for long periods, before they see the light of the day in the formulated language.

> 'Solitude is the mother of perfectability.'
> ANCIENT GREEK
> EXPRESSION

Unlike loneliness, which is felt as misery, mental anguish and the sense of abandonment by the world, solitude is the meaningful silence which we seek for its own rewards.

Listening to Silence

There are still places on this earth - in the villages of the Andes, in the hamlets of the Himalayas, in some remote mountainous parts of Greece, where silence reverberates, where you can hear the stars singing as you observe the majesty of the Milky Way. When you are steeped in this silence, you begin to understand one of the conditions that enabled the ancient Greeks to achieve so much excellence.

> *Time is your friend. Meditate so that you are a friend to yourself.*
>
> ❦

It is hard for us to imagine that until the 19th century, or even the beginning of the 20th century, the prevailing condition of most human settlements was silence. Silence usually brings with it the sense of larger space around ourselves. If you cultivate silence, you can deliberately create a larger space around you. This is why meditation is so important. Meditation creates the space of silence; silence then creates conditions of creativity and sane living.

Listening to Silence

A Buddhist monk (previously an American soldier who chose the tranquility of the Thai monasteries over the hell of the Vietnam War) told me about his experiences with English students after he settled in Britain. He mentioned to me that many British students are aware of the thinness and triviality of the knowledge they receive at universities. Subconsciously, and sometimes deliberately, they seek other sources of nourishment. So they would invite him to give talks and to lead meditations - often expecting to reach Nirvana after a single meditation. Instead my Thai Buddhist friend would ask them to sit for thirty minutes in silence - just as a beginning. They found this very difficult, just to sit for thirty minutes in silence without anybody guiding them or talking to them. These students are not an exception. We are all restless children of a restless civilization.

The Taste of Silence

The triviality of our lives and the lack of silence, and lack of space for reflection, are closely connected. In our continuous rushing we lose the silence and the meaning of our lives.

You can practice the yoga of Silence by re-discovering the good taste of silence. This is a very simple way, but it is not easy. We have allowed ourselves to consider continuous noise as normal. We have allowed ourselves to regard mental clutter as inevitable. We have lost the good habit of enjoying silence. We need to regain this habit by reclaiming clean spaces and firmly pushing away all surplus noise and clutter.

Silence is a necessary condition of recovering human meaning. The yoga of Silence creates the circumstances which enable you to go to your inner springs where peace, creativity and meaning reside.

Enjoying Silence

*Persevere in solitude
and your mind will
acquire a necessary peace ;
Silence creates the
conditions of creativity
and sane living.*

At night, when the rattle of human activities is gone, sit comfortably on a chair and simply listen to silence. Savor its quality. Realize how much better you feel inside amidst silence. Drink this silence. Whenever the opportunity occurs in daily life, when you are in a quiet space - give yourself to silence, even if only for a minute or two.

Sitting without doing anything is not an idle luxury, for silence creates concentration and ultimately "creates" time, as it releases us from the merciless rushing around which is the cause of so much wasted time.

Always remember, time is your friend.

The Yoga of Listening

Perfect listening
is comprehending the
singing of the universe.
Particular human
narratives are fragments
of melodies in the great
cosmic symphony.

The Yoga of Listening

arlier on our journey we looked at the importance of reverence for nature, and for ourselves. Now we can apply this principle of reverence to everyone and ask ourselves what it means to treat other humans reverentially.

Most of our communion with others happens through language. Language can be deceitful or empty but it is still the most powerful bond that ties human beings. The art of listening is subtle and important.

Listening is an acknowledgement of the other. Listening is embracing the other person in a field of empathy, an expression of true reverence for another person. We must listen to the unspoken word as well as to the spoken. When two lovers are together they have an exquisite capacity to listen to each other, to their words and to the silence in which they are enveloped. We can all strive to attain that level of perfect listening.

Listening is an art that we can acquire with practice, when we understand its extraordinary subtlety.

The Art of Listening

Jesus was a good listener. Days before the Last Supper, there was a sense of tension among his followers, an ominous awareness of bad things to come. Women from a local village brought perfumes and other sweet oils to anoint Jesus. Some disciples turned angrily toward the women, accusing them of frivolity in spending their precious money on unnecessary things. Yet Jesus knew better. He told the disciples to leave them alone, for the women came to do something very important for themselves.

King Lear, on the other hand, did not have the capacity to listen. He gullibly accepted the shameless flattery of Goneril and Regan. When it was Cordelia's turn she came with her heart full of love, but with her lips sealed. When asked, "What do you promise?" she replied: "Nothing." The enraged, unlistening fool of a king shouted, "Nothing will come of nothing." So he denounced his daughter and she was forced into exile. The poor fool Lear later died in misery.

The Yoga of Listening

The yoga of Listening is controlling your ego so that it does not only hear what it wants to hear. The yoga of Listening is not crushing your ego, it is an act of enlarging your greater self. Listening is a property of human beings. Its beauty lies in our ability to tune in perfectly to the music of another.

There is a great sense of joy in two people conjoined in the communion of talking and listening to each other. Some extraordinary mystery occurs when people listen well to each other. In providing the space of freedom to others, you contribute to this great mystery.

Good listening is ultimately a form of love. When we listen well we not only celebrate the other but we also celebrate ourselves. ❧

The first thing in listening well is to decide to listen well... and then listen well. Be present. Be compassionate. Create space for the other. Create space for yourself.

Learn to Listen Well

In the act of good listening much more is involved than knowledge of the subject matter. Listening is an act of beholding another as sacred. Yes, knowledge is important. But beyond knowledge there is discernment and wisdom. Discernment is in fact a consequence of wisdom. The wiser you are the better you can listen. Cultivate your wisdom and depth so that you can listen well.

Beyond Words

When we listen carefully, we listen not only to the language, but also to the context of the other person's speech. Reconstructing this context is not an easy matter for it sometimes involves knowing more and seeing deeper than the other person is conveying. At this point listening is like a process of building a sculpture with the other person's help. They provide the various fragments, we put them together. This is particularly apparent when we listen to a small child. Beyond the words there is a whole context of which we are more aware than the child. For this reason we can understand the child's words and vague clues better than he/she can. We know better and deeper the whole context.

Listening to children requires patience, presence, sympathy, knowing the context better than the child, and listening for the sake of the child. Perhaps we should consider listening to children as the paradigmatic case of all good listening. We do not want to treat others condescendingly, but we do want to express our reverence for adults and children by the way we listen to them.

Beyond Words

When you reconstruct the context of another person's speech you acknowledge where the other person "is coming from". His or her history is woven into their respective words, as well as the history of their cultures, and perhaps even the history of the entire world - for all is connected in one Cosmic Web.

Perhaps this god-like listening is not available to us humans. Yet by reflecting on its nature and considering its qualities we become aware of what our best listening may become - a form of comprehension that borders on the Divine.

Take care in the ways in which you listen to others. Be present with the other person and not with your thoughts and troubles and worries; for this immediately emanates to the other person. Have time for the other person; don't count your minutes and seconds for this makes you impatient and a bit absent, and this again transmits to the other person.

Create a field of sympathetic energy for the other; create the space in which the other is welcome; make the other person feel safe and at home.

Do not listen only to words but to the whole being of the person. Identify with the person as you listen. This is the yoga of Empathy. You identify this time not with a rock but with the universe of the other person.

Listen to what the other person is saying or is trying to say, and not to what you want to hear. Listening is always a selective process. Out of an extraordinary number of clues we pick up some and decipher them, but so often we decipher them according to what we want to hear.

Do not presume that you know what the other person wants to say before s/he says so.

Be aware of the flow of language as the other person speaks. If there are some interruptions or irregularities of language, this may mean that the person wants to say something different than s/he is actually saying. You probably want to return to these moments later.

Look into the other person's eyes while you listen. But not all the time for this makes many people uneasy or embarrassed. Look at the lips most of the time, for this is where speech comes from. By looking at the lips you are taking the words from the person's heart. Yet, from time to time, look into the other person's eyes. Learn from your own experience.

Reflect on the instances when you listened best. Try to reconstruct the frame of mind which enabled you to listen well. Re-create this frame of mind when you listen in the future.

'Where is the wisdom
we have lost
in knowledge?
Where is the knowledge
we have lost in
information?'

T.S. ELIOT

The Energy Addiction

We are a very powerful civilization. Yet we are weak and disempowered individuals. The power of our weapons staggers the imagination. The power of our household gadgets is equally formidable. We are witnessing a dizzying spectacle of power in the outside world and a sorry spectacle of disempowered people lost in a jungle of technology.

Why, amidst this abundance of power do we, as individuals, feel so powerless? We need to understand this problem in order to understand deeper the nature of our civilization. We also need to understand for a practical reason: we want to live a life of dignity, therefore we must not allow ourselves to become incapacitated or paralyzed.

The yoga of Empowerment is a strategy which enables us to safeguard the paths to other yogas by removing rubble and obstacles from our ways. We need some strategies to combat the numerous and insidious impediments that try to make our lives into continuous obstacle courses. These strategies and techniques outline the yoga of Empowerment.

Towards Empowerment

When we talk about empowerment we are not considering power over others but empowering ourselves to lead a life of quality. The idea of "power" in the context of empowerment has nothing to do with brute domination over others. We do not want to join the club of power-mongers who are mesmerized by the illusions of physical power, while themselves so often powerless in a genuine sense. This current concept of power, which means the power to coerce, the power over things and over people in order to control them, is really a corruption and a pathology.

Ivan Illich, one of the most perceptive critics of the pitfalls of our civilization, demonstrated in *Energy and Equity*, (1974) the perils of using too much energy per capita. Up to a certain point, the increased use of energy contributes to our individual well-being and to social cohesion and equity. But beyond this point the story is different, we become energy gluttons, energy addicts. We become so dependent on energy that gradually we lose our independence.

Encourage Self-Reliance

The more energy we use, the more gadgets we use. The more gadgets we use, the less self-reliant we become. Our gadgets simply turn into our crutches. Technological civilization encourages an extreme specialization. There is a gadget for every simple function we want to perform, and there are specialists for various gadgets. We are encouraged to think that beyond our narrow expertise, we are incompetent to do anything. Thus an excessive reliance on gadgets combined with an excessive drive toward specialization disengages us from life. Gradually and methodically this process thoroughly disempowers us.

> *Life is wonderfully versatile*
> *and extremely competent in*
> *doing everything for itself.*

Slowly try to regain your sovereignty and your self-reliance. Don't allow yourself to be persuaded that you are incapable, and that everything must be done for you by specialists. Try to use simple gadgets. Better still, try not to use them unless you must. Try not to use your car - unless necessary. Walking is so good for you, for your health, for the moments of meditation in which you may engage when you pass a beautiful flower, or a beautiful pair of eyes.

Using simple things over which you have control is empowering. Not using countless devices, which actually clutter your life, is empowering. Walking and biking whenever you can is empowering. Making your life simpler is empowering.

The Idols of the Marketplace

n the 17th century Francis Bacon was already alarmed that people were being so manipulated by current opinions and dogmas. He identified four idols of the marketplace - forces which muzzle the intellect and attempt to subjugate freedom of thought. These idols were the demands of authority, of prejudice, of the status quo, and of those who desire power over others. Today the power of the idols of the marketplace has not diminished but immensely increased, and this power is more manipulative and more insidious than ever.

One idol today, particularly in the western world, is television, and the mass media in general. The influence of television is enormous, yet we seem to be helpless to do anything about it. Many people today allow television to devour their freedom, their time and their lives. The mass media combine to create a force that wants to control, not to be controlled. They work diligently on us all. In the eyes of the media we are all prospective consumers or mere ciphers waiting to be manipulated at will.

Malign Influences

We tend to think that we are independent beings, unique individuals with our own ways of thinking and doing, but in fact many of us are enormously influenced by the media. We can scarcely avoid being influenced since we live in a social world. The question is, by whom do we allow ourselves to be influenced? Are we influenced by Mahatma Gandhi or by some slippery salesman trying to sell us an electric toothbrush, an unhealthy pudding or a shiny new car? We must make conscious choices concerning the ways we are influenced, and by whom.

> 'To differ from the multitude in thought and action is the sign of the superior person.'
> TIBETAN BUDDHIST SAYING

We must not be confused by the plethora of ambiguities and half-truths which television is so good at. Instead, we should demand that the most influential social institutions of our times serve human purposes, not the purposes of disempowering us.

Regaining the Meaning of Life

The purpose of yoga is to infuse meaning and dignity into your life, to live meaningfully in this day and age. Empowerment in our times is a form of responsibility for the life of the planet and for our own lives.

When seeking paths of empowerment we need to be clear about the nature of good and evil. We want to regain our meaning and dignity, for this reason we cannot be tolerant about everything. We cannot agree that anything goes. We make our stand for the sanctity of life, for reverence of all life. Our basic moral premise is that what is life-enhancing in the long run, is good. Whatever undercuts the vital roots of life, is evil. We all have an intuitive knowledge of right and wrong, if we allow ourselves to recognize this. We are aware that it can be difficult to make decisions and judgments on these matters, but we do have a clear perspective about what is good for all life in the long run. We must rely on our intuitions and insights. We must practice the yoga of Life through our fierce allegiance to the beauty of life.

Life is Harmony

'Who rightly with
necessity complies
In things Divine,
we count him
skilled and wise.'

EURIPIDES

Striving for Harmony

The ancient Greeks were a remarkable people. They introduced to the world democracy and philosophy, unforgettable tragedies and unsurpassed works of art. They were also artists of life, they knew how to live - in joy and with depth. They were aware of the Divine forces of the universe and also aware of the inner-god which lies dormant within us all.

Although they did not use the term yoga, they evolved distinctive strategies of life for which the term yoga would be quite appropriate. They devleloped specific techniques and concepts they valued as overall organizing principles. The most important principle of all was harmony.

This principle was seen as underlying all the universe, all art, all human endeavors. To be accomplished and wise was to understand this overall harmony, weaving yourself into its patterns. It was to conduct your life and thoughts in a harmonious way, thus enabling your life and work to possess truth, goodness, and quality. This principle was the guiding force which enabled the Greeks to see their lives as related to the overall harmony of the Cosmos.

Health and Harmony

Health was also seen as a matter of harmony within the body, and of the body with all the other energies of the universe. To envisage health in this perspective required an all embracing mind. The perspective of the mind is important, for it provides the guiding principles which make things coherent, lucid and harmonious.

Another organizing principle of the universe of the ancient Greeks was arete- conceived as striving for perfection, for excellence, for the ultimate limits of human achievement. The Greeks tried to achieve perfection, arete, in order to express the everlasting harmony. Arete can be seen as striving to reach the limits of human perfectability. It was an expression of beauty, of goodness, of integrity, of quality, and the Greeks took the idea of arete with great seriousness and verve. The Greek way of life was the practice of the yoga of Arete. This is the foundation of the greatness of the Greek culture.

> *'Health -*
> *a consummated love*
> *affair of the organs*
> *of the body.'*
>
> PLATO

Strive for Creativity

We need to reflect a little deeper why our very powerful civilization produces so many disempowered people. The present economic system, the so-called "Free Market", thrives on "success", and haunts everybody by the idea of failure. Through homogenizing the world this system tends to reduce us to repetitive, competitive automata, enslaving us to machines - even if they may be sophisticated computers - instead of inspiring us to pursue beauty, integrity, and quality.

> *Working with your hands and your body is not only a biological necessity. It is also a form of empowerment.*
>
> ❧

Artisans, craftsmen and people shaping things with their hands are fortunate, for they have the opportunity to empower themselves as they shape things through their own will and imagination. We revive when we have opportunities to fashion things creatively, to give them a bit of our soul, to express through them our energies, dreams and aspirations.

The practice of the yoga of Arete is the practice of the yoga of Empowerment.

Outline some activities at which you are good, and practice them in the spirit of arete. These may be small things of daily life. Perhaps you will prepare a favorite dish well, or clean a room with love. To do something well and with quality is empowering, whatever the task.

Never forget that time is your friend. You have time to take care over daily tasks, to act with love and reverence. Take time to meditate daily, this is empowering.

People who do things well continually re-empower themselves. It is important for each of us to do at least certain things well.

'Having understood
your own capacities,
it is necessary to
have a definite
plan of action.'
TIBETAN BUDDHIST
SAYING

*I*mitation

*I*mitation is the capacity to repeat well what others have done, to claim as our own some of the skills of human kind. It is not aping things mindlessly but meshing the skills evolved by life and proudly claiming them as your own.

> *Imitation is the prowess and pride to join the ranks of those who have excelled.*
>
> ❧

Imitation is the most ancient of the arts of empowerment. It is a natural art. When small birds begin to fly, they imitate their parents. When lion cubs begin to hunt, they imitate their elders. When small children learn to talk, they have a delightful tendency to repeat a new word over and over with a great delight. That is how they empower themselves to speak freely later. Imitation triggers the basic skills which are latent in us all.

We learn through imitation. We go through life acquiring skills - from the rudimentary to the highly refined. We imitate accomplished masters. Imagine a visit to the workplace of a Renaissance painter: all

*I*mitation

kinds of young people would be working. Some would be mixing paints, some varnishing the frames and some would be helping the artist to execute the masterpieces.

The students would not only learn how to put the paint on the canvas but also how to express the depth of human eyes in the master's tradition. They learn through being there, through being a part of everything that is going on.

A similar process happens when a student learnsto play music with great musicians. A certain amount may be learnt from books or from listening to good music. But the best way to learn is to be with great teachers, seeing and repeating how they do it, being guided by them, acquiring the particular quality of certain sounds, learning how phrases are expressed and how to put together the architecture of a whole piece. Many of our refined skills are acquired by learning from good teachers.

Another important strategy of imitation, as part of empowerment, is taking a clue from those who are already empowered.

*I*mitation

Empowerment through imitation can also mean extending yourself to the maximum extent. For a number of years the North Wall of Eiger, in the Alps, was deemed unconquerable. Every expedition of the most accomplished climbers attempting to scale this wall failed. Most who went into the wall never returned. Then in 1934 yet another expedition of two climbers went, and this time they scaled it. From this moment on the myth of the unconquerability of Eiger vanished, and most subsequent expeditions succeeded - no doubt empowered by the first ascent.

It is a great motivating force to know that a thing can be done, and has already been done. This psychological factor is very important. What is at one point considered impossible, and paralyzing at the very thought of trying, becomes an invitation to an adventure.

Therefore empowerment through imitation can mean extending your own limits to try and match the highest possible achievements, stretching yourself beyond anything which could be considered humdrum and ordinary.

Spiritual Imitation

Imitation is also important in spiritual life. The spiritual power of a great example can be a great inspiration. *The Imitation of Christ,* the title of the book by Thomas à Kempis, encapsulates the whole idea. Monks and nuns, and lay religious people, often derive their energy and sustenance by following the example of an illustrious one, be it Christ, the Buddha, or Zarathustra.

'*Study compassionately the teachings of great sages of all ages.*'

TIBETAN BUDDHIST SAYING

Following an example of a great one is empowering, it persuades us that a certain spiritual path is possible. The imitation of saints and illustrious beings empowers us to recognize our spiritual potential. However, once we have recognized this potential, we cannot blindly imitate others, for we have to find our own ways forward.

Visualization

The power of visualization is the power of the mind. It is a form of day-dreaming which, through a strange alchemy that occurs between mind and reality, can transform imagination into reality. How this happens is a bit of a mystery, but there are many important things that we do not know. We should cherish and celebrate mystery, rather than be afraid of it.

> 'The most beautiful thing we can
> experience is the mysterious.
> It is the source of all true art and science.
> He to whom this emotion is a stranger,
> who can no longer pause to wonder and
> stand wrapped in awe, is as good as dead:
> His eyes are closed.'
>
> ALBERT EINSTEIN
>
>

Visualize Empowerment

It has been found and affirmed by therapists that visualization may be a very significant factor in combatting some diseases. For example, a patient with cancer may be asked to imagine, literally to visualize, his blood cells eating cancer cells.

Visualization must be practiced with power and intensity - a patient must actually eat cancer cells with his mind. In many cases this process, when performed with great application and determination, has led to remarkable results. The states of our mind can influence and alter the states of our body, including the chemistry of some of our body processes.

We can use visualization in our daily lives. One strategy is to imagine, in concrete palpable terms, the positive outcome of what you want to accomplish. See it so very clearly - in your mind. It is there. Done. Then take those necessary steps in reality to bring your vision to fruition. You have to have courage and determination to visualize the positive outcome - as well as the steps leading to it.

Visualize Empowerment

Visualization may be disempowering when you are gripped by fear, negative feelings, uncertainty, weakness of the heart. Then you start imagining that you cannot succeed, that you must fail; you actually see yourself as having failed. Then you do not help yourself; you actually hinder yourself by bringing through visualization the negative outcome of your activity. The stuff of mind is a subtle but potent force.

It may not always seem easy but you can always be positive. There are risks involved, and you may not always succeed, but you must create in your mind the best positive scenario to help yourself to succeed.

> *Do not look for failure. Always envisage success.*
> ❦

Visualization means calling on your inner powers which are ready to help you if you are in need, and if you treat them well. You need to be friendly with those forces. They are a part of you.

Visualize Empowerment

Turning Adversity into Advantage

We try to plan our lives with care, but inevitably there are some times when things fall apart. This may be due to some events in the outside world, or because of our own slips, or, most likely, a combination of the two. We feel overrun, undone, helpless, and disempowered. This has happened to everybody.

In every unfortunate situation, we can either give in and despair; or we may use the misfortune to test our resolve and imagination.

> *There is no need to be stressed, forlorn, or miserable inside. You can Walk in Beauty.*
>
> ❧

The best resolve is to turn adversity into advantage. In doing so, we consciously redesign our situations in such a way that what threatened to be a dark spot to haunt us later becomes a bright spark and a memory that makes us smile.

Taking Positive Action

A simple example of turning a bad situation to your advantage is to imagine that you have just missed a train. You feel annoyed with yourself and the whole world. However, it is useless and disempowering to remain in this negative space, so take some positive action.

Take a deep breath, and let your smile come to your lips. Breathe deeply. You may suddenly remember that you have meant to write a letter for days and days - it has been sitting on your mind and heart, but you haven't got around to it. So do it now! You write the letter with verve and depth of feeling. It will be a memorable one - for you and the person who is going to receive it. This is turning adversity into advantage. Instead of caving in and bemoaning your fate, you will create something unexpected and extraordinarily good.

In every unfortunate situation we can give in and despair, but we may use the misfortune to test our resolve and imagination.

Centering yourself

We all desire equanimity of mind, peace and harmony. Such things cannot be purchased but you can bring them out from within yourself - if you go deep enough into yourself.

Living in a stressful environment does not help. Having a stressful occupation, which wears you down daily, does not help. You must try as best you can to choose your environment and your occupation so that they help you in gaining and maintaining your equilibrium.

In our busy and involved lives we may not seem to have a choice of which environment to dwell in, and which occupation to enter. These matters are thrust upon us. Yet we have much more choice than we usually exercise. But we must be more determined in our choices!

There are some simple techniques which can help to center you, bring back your balance and a modicum of serenity - even amidst the hectic pace of our present times. You may not have the right conditions for proper meditation, but you can always find a few seconds of time to breathe deeply.

Breathe deeply, especially when you are a bit rushed, feel rattled or overwhelmed.

Stop time and breathe deeply. While you breathe, let your smile come to your lips.

Begin to smile while you breathe. Then realize how much your face and your mind have loosened - while you breathe and smile. Let this smile spread throughout your body. Breathe and smile with your entire body.

A great magic of peace is generated by your lips as you begin to smile. Practice this smile and breathing daily. Notice how much this smile helps your well-being; and how much it helps others - when you are in a serene mood, after you have breathed and smiled.

There is a power in your smile - the power of peace and inner equilibrium. Activate this power daily, it costs you nothing! This inner tranquility is part of building your confidence, is part of your self-empowerment.

Spritual Strength

The purpose of
every yoga is not
physical fitness
but spiritual strength,
ultimately leading to
self-realization of the
individual in the
deepest sense.

Participation

With every action we perform in this world, we participate. Even if we do nothing, our body participates in countless cycles, and our mind is ticking away about so many things. The whole universe is one stupendous participatory process.

Participation is one of the primary modes of acquiring empowerment. When growing boys joined a group of hunters in old societies, this was for them a form of empowerment. Participation is so important in our lives and so common that we forget its significance. Too often we take it for granted and neglect to develop its latent potential.

There are all sorts of ways to participate. Playing trivial games with other people is participation. Choosing a box of detergent or a box of cereal among many different kinds is exercising your choice, which is a form of participation. But these are trivial participations. Watching lazy bits of news on television is a form of participation. But again, it is a trivial form of participation.

If you participate in too many trivial games and activities you will become trivialized in the end.

Participation

Trivial participation ultimately bores you, leaves behind a sense of shallowness, contributes little to your deeper sense of life. Significant participation, on the other hand, engages you, enthralls and satisfies you, it contributes to the meaning of your life.

Nearly all participation occurs in some kind of context, which is governed by rules. We are usually aware of the rules of the game and we participate in the game because in spite of the rules we can exert our prowess, show our intelligence, manifest something of our being.

> *Real participation is a manifestation of the exuberance of life.*
> ❦

Unsatisfactory forms of participation are those in which hidden rules control and manipulate others. We are frustrated in such circumstances because we are led to believe that we participate, but it is pseudo-participation.

Participation

If we are continually controlled and manipulated, life in us is thwarted. It is as simple as that. Significant participation requires that you partake actively. If you are creative, in any field or endeavor, especially the arts, you exert your intelligence and ultimately involve your soul.

> *Truly creative participation is singing with the universe.*
>
> ❧

Every positive transformation in the universe has occured as the result of creative participation. Lack of such participation can only lead to increased malaise and stagnation.

We must be aware of the context of our participation. The deeper and more significant the context, the more significant the form of participation. The shallower the context the shallower the participation - and the shallower your life.

o much in our life is empowering.and must be recognized as such. Hope is empowering. Hope is a life-force, when hope dwindles, empowerment is undermined. Responsibility is empowering. Enlightenment is empowering. Joy is empowering. Great ideas are pregnant with positive energy. You can take these ideas and make them a part of your universe.

Conceiving the world as a sanctuary is empowering. Striving for arete is empowering. Self-confidence and the sense of your own self worth is empowering. It is the certainty that you can do what you wish to, and that you are a marvellous part of the Cosmos. Wisdom is empowering. Prayer can be empowering, but not one in which you ask an outside deity to give you this or that, but one in which you raise yourself to the level of Divinity and converse with the Divine within about important matters.

Love is empowering. It is a blessed condition to be able to love, and a privileged condition to be loved.

Walking in Beauty is empowering. You can walk in beauty. This idea is empowering.

Empower yourself

If you constantly contemplate the Divine aspects of the world and try to make your life congruent with these aspects, you move towards Divinity. Remember, karma is all pervading. As you think so you become. As you participate so you carve your destiny.

The strategies of empowerment should not be considered as independent processes but one process of tuning up the entire field of your life-energy.

We must all attempt to embark on those journeys in which our creative participation is of the essence. To empower yourself is to pay tribute to the creative forces of the universe which reside within you, which want to be released and blossom.

> 'He who thinks
> of God
> becomes God,
> He who denies God
> denies hinself.'
>
> UPANISHADS

'Never did the eye see the sun
unless it had become sun-like,
and never can soul see Beauty
unless itself be beautiful.'

PLOTINUS

Finding your Spiritual Path

We are what we are. And we should not try to do violence to ourselves by attempting to be somebody else. Yet we are in the process of continuous becoming. If we stop this process, we petrify. Our creative nature, our capacity to unfold, is the most essential characteristic of our human nature. In this sense, life is a perpetual revolution, a constant re-creation of yourself.

> *Have the courage to claim your spiritual destiny.*

This is particularly true of our spiritual life, the part of life which is deepest and most meaningful. We all have a sense of what we could be spiritually and what we would like to be. This requires holding a larger view of the universe as well as holding right faith. Fanatical beliefs in limited ideologies are not the same as right faith.

Finding Your Spiritual Path

A right faith is rooted in great spiritual ideals of humanity which can sustain us all.

To pursue the Yoga of Spiritual Life you need strong faith in the Divine nature of the universe; whether it is a faith in a personal God or some large spiritual ideals uplifting to the human spirit. You need the will to make something of your own life. Everyone needs a vessel for love. So choose a spiritual path which is suitable for you.

> *To be fully human is to be Divine.*

You must not be be afraid of the Divine, for this is a force which drives us upward and also makes us sublime. You cannot leave your Divinity on the side, or you are leaving your humanity on the side.

Build Yourself into a Beautiful Being

Be courageous and explicit in calling from within your-self the person who you potentially are, the person you want to become.

Visualize all the features you would possess as that person. Imagine how you would behave, what words you would speak, what thoughts and feelings you would have if you were this person.

Then create for yourself a plan to acquire your desired features. You are now like a sculptor chiselling a statue in marble. Visualize the various aspects of the person you are to become and slowly but deliberately incorporate them into your being.

Take time, you cannot rush this process, but you can return to it again and again.

Your Perfect Being

'Withdraw into yourself and look.
And if you do not find yourself beautiful yet,
do as does the creator of a statue that is to be
made beautiful; he cuts away here, smoothes there,
he makes this line lighter, this other purer, until
he has shown a beautiful face upon his statue.
So do you also; cut away all that is excessive,
straighten all that is crooked, bring light to all
that is shadow, labor to make all glow with beauty,
and do not cease chiselling your statue until
there shall shine out on you the godlike splendour
of virtue, until you shall see the final goodness
surely established in the stainless shrine.
And when you have made this perfect work...
call up all your confidence, strike forward
yet a step - you need a guide no longer.'

PLOTINUS

The Journey

acred books of all cultures are signposts which guide us on the journey towards spiritual satisfaction. But you need to find your own path, as you make this journey alone. You need to become comfortable with your spiritual nature, with your inner god. You need to have empathy for your inner Divinity; at least as much empathy as you have for the elements of nature with which you identify: the rock, the soil, the running water, the tree.

By bathing in the energy and qualities of the Divine, you

> *'Awake, arise!*
> *Strive for the*
> *highest, and be*
> *in the light!'*
>
> UPANISHADS

slowly approach the Divine - while creating a reverential space within yourself. In the Hindu scripture there is a wonderful term: "Brahmavidya" - the capacity to see the Divine. We all have this capacity, we must not ignore it.

The Divine Kingdom

The Divine Kingdom is open to you, if you dare to enter it. You need a great deal of resolve and discipline and you need to do a great deal of work on yourself. When you are ready, this kingdom is prepared to allow you in. Then it will take you in quite naturally.

In order to enter this kingdom you must dare to do so, you must have the will to do so, and you must empower yourself to continue with the quest. Above all, you must link yourself with the highest light and become it. You need to use the techniques of visualization and visualize that you are already there. Then you can make that Divine space into the palpable reality around you. You will need great faith.

Beware that you do not become too dependent on any master or guru. They point a direction. Their role is to help you to liberate yourself. When you are set forth on the right path, you alone can reach enlightenment. A teacher should empower you to become your own master, not to follow others.

You are responsible for your own spiritual destiny, you must negotiate the sublime peaks yourself.

*U*ltimate *L*iberation

here is an innermost center in us all where truth and peace and light reside. The distance to this center is short, but the time to reach it is long. Have you started this journey? Are you becoming more friendly with the universe, with time, with other people, with yourself? Are you becoming more forgiving? More luminous inside?

We have a multitude of choices in front of our eyes, and in front of our minds: ancient knowledge, contemporary knowledge, esoteric knowledge. How does anyone choose what is right and appropriate? You need to be enlightened to make enlightened choices. To begin with, you need to take yourself seriously. But we do not mean that you should become a pompous ass, full of gas and self-importance. To take yourself seriously is to attempt to realize your potential.

> *'Not I, nor anyone else can travel that road for you. You must travel it yourself.'*
>
> WALT WHITMAN

Recapture your Divinity

You can never recapture
your Divinity if you never
assume that you are Divine.
To take yourself seriously is to
aspire to become Divine -
without hallucination,
without megalomania,
without losing your balance,
but by following a sane path,
which becomes a path of grace
and ultimately the path
of Divinity.

At the beginning was light. And all there is, is made of light - from the primordial photons of the Big Bang. You are made of light. Life is light manifested in the plethora of forms.

Imagine yourself to be light in various manifestations and transformations.

Feel your being, your bones, flesh and blood, filled with light, radiating with light.

Walking, sleeping, dreaming- know yourself as light.

Imagine the Cosmos as an eternal translucent presence. Feel luminous!

Imagine all of space slowly absorbed into your own head. Bring the light of the universe to reside in your head. Do it gently.

Remain in this luminous state for a while. Very slowly come back.

Life is Supreme

Life is supreme.
Life is a multitude of
colors of the rainbow.
We don't need to be stressed,
forlorn, feeling miserable inside.
We can walk in beauty.
You can walk in beauty!
But first you need to take
yourself seriously as a special
atom of grace in this universe.

Inner Peace

Those balancing acts of keeping your mind clear, of keeping your desk clear, of keeping your health in good shape - what are they for? Their purpose is to keep your inner self in the state of contentment.

Inner happiness is the most important thing. It is the source of true happiness. All other forms of happiness: the material gratification, the state of sensual satisfaction, the recognition by other people - are all of secondary importance, are trivial in comparison with inner peace and inner contentment.

Like the saints and spiritual seekers, you don't want to be satisfied with what's only on the surface. You want a true happiness, which is a spiritual bliss. For this reason, you keep your house in order. You tidy your outer spaces so that your inner space is not disturbed and continually cluttered. This act is very simple, but very difficult in our times where clutter is the order of the day.

You lead a simple life for the sake of spiritual bliss, not for the sake of leading a simple life.

Inner Peace

What is the price of inner peace, of contentment, of happiness? Can you afford the time for reaching happiness and attaining inner peace? Or would you rather squander your time on insignificant trivia, and then complain that you have no time to work on yourself?

You need to face this question squarely: How do you want to spend your life? The choice is yours, but this is not an ordinary choice, it is a choice of your destiny. To make the right choice you need clarity of perception, and clarity of vision, so you see whether your daily activities enlighten you, ennoble you, give you the strength to see and the wings to fly. This clarity of vision is there - inside you. Dig deep. Don't be afraid of your depth. It is your best friend.

There is nothing for nothing. You want your inner peace and happiness so you need time and discipline. You also need splendid resolve, a determination which will inform you that you are going to make something of your life, that your life is important, that you do take yourself seriously as a spiritual person.

Indian Prayer

Oh great spirit
Whose voice I hear in the winds,
And whose breath gives life to all the world,
Hear me! I am small and weak,
I need your strength and wisdom

Let me walk in beauty, and make my eyes
Ever behold the red and purple sunset.

Make my hands respect the things you have made
And my ears sharp to hear your voice.

Indian Prayer

Make me wise so that I may understand
The things you have taught my people.

Let me learn the lessons you have hidden
In every leaf and rock.

I seek strength, not to be greater than my brother,
But to fight my greatest enemy - myself.

Make me always ready to come to you
With clean hands and straight eyes.

So when life fades, as the fading sunset,
My spirit may come to you without shame.

Ecological Spirituality

The yoga of Spiritual Life does assume that the universe is pervaded with Divinity and that you are a Divine speck yourself. It does not assume that your spiritual life must be tied to some form of organized religion or God-centered religion.

The yoga of Spiritual Life is a part of EcoYoga. It is therefore quite natural that within Eco-Yoga we shall come to recognize ecological spirituality. This spirituality is distinctive, and it helps us to live in this epoch, which is the ecological epoch.

As we have said, to act in the world as if it were a sanctuary is to make it reverential and sacred.

> *Embrace the stars so that they give you strength to maintain your resolve.*

What the universe becomes depends on you. Treat it like a machine and it becomes a machine. Treat it like a Divine place and it becomes a Divine place. Reverence for life, and for all there is in the universe, is the first condition of ecological spirituality.

Ecological Spirituality

A deep comprehension of ecology is reverence in action, is a deep identification with the beauty of life pulsating through the universe until we become part of it. Thus understanding becomes empathy. Empathy becomes universal reverence. This reverence is a form of spirituality. In our times the ecological and the spiritual become one. This is the foundation of ecological spirituality.

Healing the earth is the spiritual work of our time.

❦

Healing the planet and healing ourselves is spiritual work of the first magnitude in our day and age. Whatever may be our race and religion, ecology binds us all together. Ecology is the universal religious project of our times. The idea of redemption acquires a new meaning - it means redeeming the world by healing the earth. We need to emphasize: To understand religious devotion is to recognize that all religions are forms of worship of the beauty and integrity of the planet.

Ecological Spirituality

Spirituality is also, and has always been, the realization of our inner potential, the actualization of the inner god within us. We need to treat each other according to what we could potentially become: Divine lights uplifting ourselves and helping others to heal, to integrate, to become more reverential.

Working on ourselves to release and articulate our inner Divinity and working in the outside world to heal the earth are the complementary aspects of ecological spirituality.

Thus ecological spirituality connects our care for the earth with our concern for our inner selves. Reverence for the earth merges with reverence for the god-within.

> *'It is a great joy that the spirit of all living beings is inseparable from the universal spirit.'*
> TIBETAN BUDDHIST
> SAYING

By practicing right yogas well we participate in the great liturgy in which the Cosmos is revered by our reverential mind.

Smile with Your Body

Sit comfortably in a place where you can be assured of three to five minutes of peace. You are going to walk in beauty - with your entire being.

Close your eyes. Breathe deeply. Smile with your mind. You can! Smile again. Let this smile come to your lips, and from your lips let this smile spread to your eyes and cheeks and your whole face. Now smile with your neck and then with your entire spine - one vertebra after another. Smile with your entire back. Extend this smile to your stomach, your kidneys, your liver. May this smile engulf your ribs and fill your lungs.

Smile with your beautiful heart; Let your smile go up to your shoulders and down your arms... right through your palms and fingers! And your smile works its way down through your legs, your thighs and knees and ankles. and feet and heels and toes.

Now your entire body is beautifully relaxed, As you smile with your entire body, greet the universe and embrace it with your smiling energy.

The Inner Springs of Life

'To treat man

as he is

Is to debase him;

To treat man

as he ought to be

Is to engrace him.'

GOETHE

New Departures are Possible

In any human enterprise, small or big, new departures are possible. When you radically depart from the old, you have to have the vision to imagine new things. Also, you have to have the will to follow through your vision. You need vision to guide your will; you need will to sustain your vision.

From the hidden springs of our inspiration, from the deeper reservoir of our values and ultimate visions, there comes an insight telling us to do something new because it is good and worth doing. This vision, which arrives from the hidden springs of intuition, provides potency and creative substance. Only later comes the rational process which justifies this vision - which is a tribute the mind pays to the deep insight of vision.

Original thinking precedes rationalization. Yet this form of thinking requires the courage of non-conformity. Courage plays a paramount role in any form of original thinking. Without courage nothing can be accomplished.

In order to shake off the dust of the old and to overcome the inertia of things that do not work but

New Departures are Possible

want to stay, you must have the freedom of imagination. Imagination is another word for vision. You need staggering imagination to overcome the rut of the paralyzing old order of things.

'We must never lose infinite hope.'

MARTIN LUTHER KING

You also need monumental hope. You need hope to give wings to courage, and courage to renew the energy of hope.

Each of these concepts connects with the other three. Together vision, will, hope and courage form a deep structure of human action - the structure which is pre-rational or trans-rational, but which, at the same time justifies all our rational pursuits. These inner springs of life form a circular mandala in which each element co-defines the other three.

Hope is the scaffolding of our very being. To be alive is to live in the state of hope. Hope is a precondition of our mental health and of our physical health. Hope is not a spurious trapping, not a luxury, but the very fountain of inner life.

*H*ope

*H*ope is a re-assertion of our belief in the meaning of human life; and in the sense of the universe. Hope is a pre-condition of all meaning, of all strivings, of all actions. To embrace hope is a form of wisdom; to abandon it is a form of foolishness.

Hope is the nourishment that sustains us daily, the oxygen for our hearts and souls. Hope is the very ray of light that separates life from death. The logic of hope is the logic of affirmation and of solidarity. It is the logic of

> *Hope sustains love,*
> *while love*
> *sustains hope.*
>
> ❧

compassion and of courage. The logic of hope is also the logic of responsibility. All these attributes are the very stuff of which life is made: the life which is alive, radiant, peaceful and harmonious.

Hope is courage, and courage is not blind. Hope is affirmation, and affirmation is not stupid. Hope is responsibility, and responsibility excludes ventures that are crazy or utterly impossible.

Hope and Courage

The logic of hope gives us the permission to be and to become in the image of our spiritual self, in the image of the person we ought to be. Hope is claiming back the better part of ourselves. Living in hope is a good yoga. Hope sustains love, while love sustains hope.

> *Courage fuels hope while hope gives wings to courage.*
>
> ❧

It takes courage to live life as an authentic being, not as an automaton manipulated by social dictates or biological urges, but a free agent who makes painful choices Without courage we cannot live meaningfully. When our faith in the meaning of life crumbles, what saves it is an act of courage which infuses us with the power and determination to continue onwards.

Courage is the fuel which renews the energy of hope. Courage and hope are twin sisters. Courage is not in the domain of mind or pure rationality. Nor is it in the domain of the heart or pure emotions.

Courage

Courage is a hidden dimension of our existence, which supports our quest for meaning. Courage is the necessity of the human condition. Without courage we cannot write poetry, conceive new philosophy, think up new scientific theories. Every new departure of human spirit or mind is an act of courage.

Courage fuels our action and our imagination. Those who don't have enough courage, clip the wings of their imagination. Imagination or vision is the courage of dreaming new things, extraordinary things, great things. New ideas will not visit our mind unless we have the courage to dream them up. The same holds for our personal lives. If you never imagine yourself as a courageous person who can accomplish things and claim for yourself a life of dignity and beauty, you will not arrive at the life of dignity and beauty.

> *Courage is subtle and untouchable . like a passing wind - yet it touches all.*
> ❦

Courage

In silence and courage we conceive new worlds. In the middle of our faltering life there emerges an act of courage which prompts and encourages us to go on even if everything might seem utterly absurd.

Courage is part of the process of empowerment, and a hidden source of this empowerment.

❧

One enemy of courage is fear, which makes you small, which forces you to retreat into your pitiful little shell. Another enemy of courage is the memory of past failures. You feel afraid because you have failed in the past, and you have failed in the past because you didn't have enough courage - the courage to persevere; the courage and determination to go out, to turn adversity into advantage.

To have courage does not mean never to fail; but to get up, shake off the dust, smile and go forward, persevere, and try again.

The Inner Springs of Life

Vision

If you are given eyes and you never properly open them, you are half-blind. If you are given gifts of imagination and vision and never use them, you grope in darkness.

There is also a deeper truth to contemplate: as we imagine ourselves to be, so we shall become. He who thinks of God, becomes God. What we think, what we imagine ourselves as capable of being, we become.

Our visions are the wings carrying us to new realms and realities. This process of envisioning and imagining is a part of the strategy of visualization.

> *'To the eye of the man*
> *of Imagination*
> *Nature is imagination itself.*
> *As man is, so he sees.'*
>
> WILLIAM BLAKE
>
>

Vision

By projecting from within that which we wish to become, we make our journey to the sublime peaks of enlightenment.

Without vision we undergo a slow psychic death. Vision is not necessary for a hum-drum existence, but is vital for an inspired one. What plagues our society most nowadays is an atrophy of vision. Drifting, nihilism, violence - all are expressions of the desperate hunger for a positive vision.

Vision is a tremendous, priceless asset. It transcends rationality. It is god-like. The gift of vision enables us to see through all possible horizons.

'The mind filled with love and compassion, while in thought or in action, must always be directed to the service of every living being.'

TIBETAN BUDDHIST SAYING

Will

The phenomenon of will and of will-power is beyond our rational understanding. And at the same time it is totally rational. We know how it works in daily life, and how necessary it is for us to go on with daily living. Will brings to fruition our actions and our dreams.

Yet will can become a very sharp cutting sword if not used judiciously. We must avoid developing the kind of will that crushes others, bending them to our ego. We must cultivate the will that gives the form to our activities - like the potter who gives shape to the amorphous clay; the will that sustains, encourages and inspires.

To inspire others to have the will to live, to persevere, to give meaning to the amorphous substance of life - this is to be a messenger of the gods.

To be endowed with the will which enables us to live in dignity in spite of the treachery of life, this is to be worthy of the inner god that resides in us all.

Will

To possess the will that nurses
our visions and brings us
closer to the path of angels,
that infuses us with compassion
and makes us glow like
a soft amber -
that is the secret of wisdom.

The Key to Happiness

The concept of happiness as an object to attain should be abandoned, for it is a trap usually concealing an ego trip. The key to happiness is to lose your ego and ambition, and to acquire a vision and a mission. You should not strive for happiness. You can only arrive at happiness while striving for other things. Happiness is not a fixed state of being: it is a state of perpetual becoming.

Happiness is being at peace with yourself while the self is united with a larger order of things.

You should strive for the meaning in life, for the fulfillment that goes beyond your individual egoistic self. You are as great as the causes you aspire to.

Great causes elevate you and make you transcend your small self. Great causes pervade you with reverence and infuse you with dignity, which are necessary components of a worthy life. Stretch yourself to the maximum in the service of others, in the cause of altruism.

170

The Key to Happiness

Merge with the larger scheme of things by understanding that the human destiny is made of the stars and not only of ordinary clay. And then your life will be enhanced, your being enlarged. And perhaps as a by-product you will arrive at happiness.

Happiness is the equilibrium of your being which is recognized by others as a state of serenity that is inspiring and uplifting; which is felt by you as a state of inner tranquillity that gives you strength and determination; not a state of sensual satisfaction or a state of physical comfort but a state of inner radiance which you will recognize more and more as you approach it closer and closer.

The truly blessed people, the giants of human thought and spirit, did not search for happiness, yet they were undoubtedly happy. Happiness will come to you when you abandon the quest and concentrate on living your life to the full in the service of others.

Noble Impulses

The inner springs of life are part of the philosophy of affirmation and empowerment; also part of the repertoire of celebrating life. In its deepest meaning, all life is a celebratory force. The philosophy of affirmation goes against the grain of today's malaise, against the modern trends of resignation, of despondence, of disempowerment.

If you elect the philosophies of despondence and cynicism as your guides, nothing positive will follow. You disempower yourself from the beginning, and the result will be the atrophy of the meaning of life. Present cynicism, relativism and nihilism should not be benignly tolerated as an expression of the liberated, sophisticated classes. They are deadly, disempowering ideologies which extinguish our spirit and diminish the spark of life.

Life is a Celebration

Life is a celebratory event.
Let us choose the forces of
life which will safeguard
the beauty of life.
Through hope, vision,
courage and will,
we choose life which
celebrates itself.

Sensitivities as Flowers of Life

'Look carefully in an
animal at a spirit alive;
Every flower is a soul
opening out into nature;
A mystery touching love
is asleep inside metal.'

GERARD DE NERVAL

o practice EcoYoga means to recognize our place in the Cosmic order of things. We can only make sense of it all when we truly begin to understand life forces and their astonishing interaction and development. One revealing and important way in which we can comprehend evolution and life itself is through understanding the power and nature of sensitivities. Sensitivities are the subtle tentacles by which we embrace life and through which we articulate life. This is as true of lower forms of life as it is of human life.

> *Sensitivities are part of the symphony through which life sings its song.*
>
> ❧

As we go through life we develop various sensitivities, such as the capacity to listen to music or the capacity to understand the moods of people around us. We develop sensitivity to animals and to other forms of nature, to plants and trees. When the first amoebas emerged from the primordial organic soup, they were victorious because they acquired a new sensitivity enabling them to react to the environment in a semiconscious manner. This was the beginning of all learning. Learning is a capacity, a sensitivity, to react to the environment and its conditions with feedback.

> *The emergence of every new form of sensitivity is a new window on the world.*
>
>

The glory of evolution starts when organisms begin to use their capacities, their sensitivities, in a conscious and deliberate manner to further their well-being.

When matter began to sense and then evolved the eye as the organ of its new sensitivity, this was a moment of great importance. Reality could now be seen and could therefore be explained according to the power of the seeing eye. The eye brought a visual aspect to reality.

Explaining the World

The seeing ability of the eye is a form of sensitivity through which we explain reality around us. Seeing is one of many sensitivities. They are all products of the articulation of evolution. But they are not just passive repositories of the evolutionary process. Through our sensitivities we apprehend and articulate what we call reality.

> *'I feel more*
> *and more everyday*
> *as my imagination*
> *strengthens.'*
>
> JOHN KEATS

Explaining the World

With new sensitivities we explain the world in new ways. We elicit from the world new aspects. The power of sensitivities is the power of co-creation. This is an important point. You participate in so many diverse ways because you have developed countless sensitivities which make up the vehicles for participating in reality.

Sensitivity holds the key to understanding.

No aspect of reality imposes itself on us with irresistible force. We take it in and then assimilate it if, and only if, we possess an appropriate sensitivity that is capable of processing this aspect of reality for us.

By acquiring new sensitivities we acquire new powers of creation. Sensitivity does not only open the doors to our understanding of evolution, but to the understanding of ourselves. The human quest is one of acquiring ever more sensitivities. We are as deep, versatile and accomplished as the repertoire and power of sensitivities residing in us.

Truth, goodness, love, and beauty are vehicles of our sensitivity. What we call "spirituality", "the religious feeling", "the sacred", and "the Divine", are all expressions signifying an enhanced sensitivity, an enhanced capacity of the individual to react to the world and to transcend the limitations of matter.

To define the human being as a sensitive animal, as one who forms himself through the acquisition and enlargement of his sensitivities, is to pay homage to the openness of our future and to all our as yet unknown but possible attainments.

> *You are as human as you are*
> *creative, as you are free.*
> *Sensitivities are your vehicles to*
> *freedom, to creativity, and ultimately*
> *a ladder to heaven.*
>
>

Evolving the Future

The right concept of the human is one which acknowledges all our past attainments but which, at the same time, makes us open to future refinements, to the acquisitions of the power of consciousness far beyond anything we have so far attained. It is clear that our future does not depend on the invention of new technologies, but on the articulation of new sensitivities, which will make us more compassionate, more understanding, more spiritual.

We shall have to evolve new sensitivities, some of which are yet undreamed of, some of which are given to us in rudimentary forms such as telepathy. Sensitivities are the flowers of life evolving. We must cultivate right flowers so that our garden blossoms for the benefit and joy of all beings in the Cosmos.

Sensitivities and Participation

Participation is the song of creation. In order to participate you must possess the powers and sensitivities that enable you to participate fully, meaningfully, intelligently.

You must possess intelligence to participate intelligently. You must possess aesthetic sensitivities to participate in the feast of cultures and the plethora of art the cultures left behind.

You must develop spiritual sensitivities to touch the ineffable and be touched by it. The larger and more versatile the scope of your sensitivities, the larger person you become.

Write down the sensitivities which you consider your greatest assets. Contemplate how you can strengthen them, how you can use them to make your life more versatile, more radiant, simply greater.

Then move to another level. Observe which sensitivities enable you to be most creative. Your creativity is expressed through certain talents and capacities. These capacities are rooted in your sensitivities. The more developed your sensitivities (of a certain kind) the more pronounced your capacity and the more articulated your talent.

Ask yourself how you would like to develop your creativity further. Trace which sensitivities you need to develop. Notice what forms of empowerment you bring to bear in order to help to develop and refine these sensitivities.

You are not a cipher, nor are you a god. You are a struggling being in the process of becoming. You were born in the human form - and not for nothing. Birds can sing. Flowers blossom radiantly. But only you can embrace the Divine. Your Mind Divine can see in the lotus flower the smiling Buddha.

You can relive the past, and you can conjure up the future. You can make yourself into the Light Extraordinary. You can. Do not settle for anything less.

Never be less than you were created for.

Meditate on this subject at least once a week.

You are alive. You have the eyes to see, to admire the beauty of art, of nature, of yourself. You have the mind and the soul to read and enjoy poetry, and art. You have the heart to love and be loved. You have the body or the imagination to carry you wherever you wish to go - including those wonderful peaks of the highest mountains. You have amazingly dexterous hands with which you can do and create many things. You have a sense of humor. You have a voice to sing and a spirit to listen. You even have wings to fly like angels - your mind is your wings! So fly.

Do not allow yourself to be held down, but enjoy the powers of creation vested in you. You have been given all the gifts of life, so use them and enjoy them.

Freedom and Humanity

Freedom does not mean to do as you please. But genuine freedom signifies the ability to extend the scope of the possible, within the species and within yourself. This freedom can be reached through developing appropriate sensitivities.

Freedom means paying tribute to your authentic self, while you have developed this self to its limits. Freedom means reclaiming your Cosmic origins by discovering that you are marvelously connected with all living beings.

Without your sensitivities you are nothing, you are unable to appreciate the world and your place within it. Your sensitivities are the instruments through which the entire symphony of your life is played.

In order to be fully human, fully alive, you must develop your sensitivities to their full potential.

> *Freedom is reclaiming your spiritual destiny by knowing that you came from the cosmic dust but now you are the consciousness of the stars.*
>
>

All Life is Yoga

The form of our being depends on the forms of sensitivities that we incorporate into the structure of our life. The progress of our being depends on the actualization of sensitivities latent in us. We do not know how many new sensitivities evolution is still holding in store for us. But is exciting to think that many await.

As you practice various yogas, you participate in various sensitivities: you express your being through them. As you begin to follow along the foothills of enlightenment, you refine some delicate sensitivities which have always been dormant in you: compassion, unconditional love, seeing beyond the ordinary, the sense of grace which brings enormous peace.

We now end our initial journey of EcoYoga. But in many ways the journey has just begun if you are determined to make something of your life. All life is yoga, including your life. Make it a good yoga - through the meditations and exercises here provided.

Remember, the beauty of life lies in practicing beautiful living, so go forward, and practice.

Go

Go and walk on the clouds.
Dusk does not come to those
Who are friends with the stars.

Go and heal broken branches
Of trees and human hearts
The only craft you need is love.

Go

Go and cry with the rivers
Go and cry with the newly born

Each needs a warm tear
Of the eye that can see clear.

Go and sing if you can
Go and mourn if you must
The universe is right
If you are on the right path.

The Author

When holding a tree,
I am simply entranced.
I return to the protoform of my being,
My cells are renewed,
My energy recharged.
My tree — my sister, my love, my lungs.
People think me crazy holding a tree.
Deep down they envy me.
I am so rooted kissing the bark.
They are so alienated avoiding it.

When I am one with a tree
The great energy of the Cosmos
Pulsates through me.
What a delight!

Other Books by Henryk Skolimoswki

Eco-Philosophy: Designing New Tactics for Living,
Marion Boyars 1981
The Theatre of the Mind, Quest Books 1984
Dancing Sheba in the Ecological Age, Clarion Press,
New Delhi 1991
Living Philosophy: Eco-Philosophy as a Tree of Life,
Penguin Books 1992
*A Sacred Place to Dwell: Walking with Reverence upon
the Earth,* Element Books 1993
*The Participatory Mind: A New Theory of the Mind
and of the Universe,* Penguin Books 1994

Henryk Skolimowski is the founder of Eco-philosophy. He holds the Chair of Ecological Philosophy at
the University of Warsaw, Poland. He has also taught
the subject in British and American universities, and
is a Research Fellow of Columbia University, and
Professor of philosophy at the University of
Michigan. He travels widely, lecturing and giving
workshops all over the world, but makes sure he can
spend several months each year in Theologos,
Greece, which he calls his EcoYoga sanctuary.

List of full page illustrations

John Farleigh, Birch Trees 1945, page 85
Blair Hughes-Stanton, Saturn and Vesta 1934, page 13;
Creation 1937, pages 164-165; The City Rises 1934, page 117;
Rebirth 1931, page 93
Norman Janes, Landscape 1949, pages 78-79
Agnes Miller-Parker, Coquette 1941, page 175
Paul Nash, Black Poplar Pond 1922, page 31; Elms 1924,
page 49; Coronilla 1925, page 125;
Charles Nightingale, Ploughing 1922, page 39
Claughton Pellew, Marsh Marigolds 1930, page 57
Monica Poole, September Day 1971, page 157
Nora S Unwin, Teasel and Grasses 1929, page 63
All the above are © British Museum

Eric Ravilious, Device on exhibition invitation, 1933, page 69
Sergei Schwemberger, Helios 1990, page 19 © the artist
Clifford Webb, from *The Serpent's Presence,* Golden Cockerel
Press 1954, page 137
Boris Zabirokhin, Spring 1990 © the artist, page 103